Abigail Breslin

ABDO
Publishing Company

A Big Buddy Book
by **Sarah Tieck**

VISIT US AT
www.abdopublishing.com

Published by ABDO Publishing Company, 8000 West 78th Street, Edina, Minnesota 55439.

Copyright © 2009 by Abdo Consulting Group, Inc. International copyrights reserved in all countries. No part of this book may be reproduced in any form without written permission from the publisher. Buddy Books™ is a trademark and logo of ABDO Publishing Company.

Printed in the United States.

Coordinating Series Editor: Rochelle Baltzer
Contributing Editor: Marcia Zappa
Graphic Design: Maria Hosley
Cover Photograph: *AP Photo*: Evan Agostini
Interior Photographs/Illustrations: *AP Photo*: AP Photo (p. 22), Evan Agostini (p. 20), Tammie Arroyo (p. 21), Kristie
    Bull/Graylock.com (p. 11), Lee Celano (p. 13), Ric Francis (p. 27), Jennifer Graylock (p. 15), Carolyn Kaster
    (p. 12), Twentieth Century Fox/Eric Lee (p. 16), Danny Moloshok (p. 19), Chris Pizzello (pp. 18, 25), Benadette
    Tuazon (p. 5); *Clipart.com* (p. 6); *Getty Images*: Evan Agostini (p. 9), Lester Cohen/WireImage (p. 27), Frazer
    Harrison/Getty Images for AFI (p. 7), John Shearer/WireImage (p. 29), Noel Vasquez (p. 23).

Library of Congress Cataloging-in-Publication Data

Tieck, Sarah, 1976-
  Abigail Breslin / Sarah Tieck.
    p. cm. -- (Big buddy biographies)
  ISBN 978-1-60453-547-1
  1. Breslin, Abigail, 1996---Juvenile literature. 2. Actors--United States--Biography--Juvenile literature. I. Title.

PN2287.B6855T54 2009
791.4302'8092--dc22
[B]
                                        2008033515

Abigail
Breslin

Contents

Rising Star

Abigail Breslin is a talented actress. She has appeared in television shows and movies. Abigail is known for starring in *Little Miss Sunshine* and *Kit Kittredge: An American Girl*.

Abigail was nominated for an Academy Award for *Little Miss Sunshine*. Every year, these awards are presented to outstanding actors, writers, and directors.

Family Ties

Abigail Breslin was born on April 14, 1996, in New York City, New York. Her parents are Kim and Michael Breslin. She has two older brothers named Ryan and Spencer.

Abigail was named for Abigail Adams. Abigail Adams was the First Lady of the United States from 1797 to 1801.

Kim often attends events with Abigail.

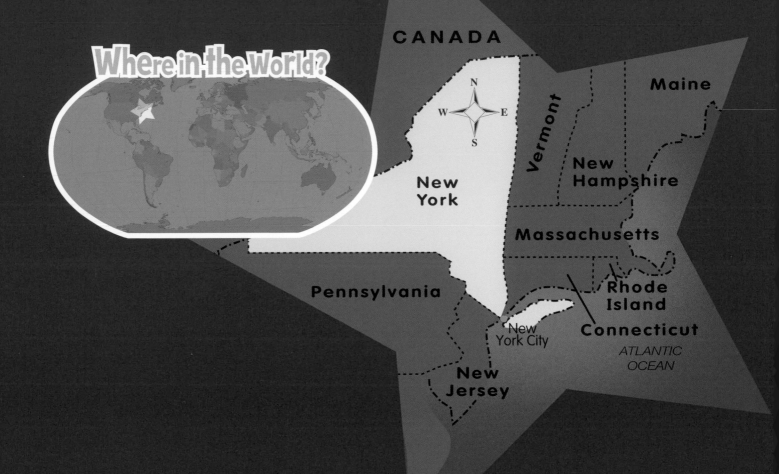

Where in the World?

CANADA

Maine

Vermont

New Hampshire

New York

Massachusetts

Pennsylvania

Rhode Island

Connecticut

New York City

ATLANTIC OCEAN

New Jersey

Abigail and her family live in an apartment in New York City. The Breslins are close. Like Abigail, Spencer is an actor. Kim works as their manager. Michael works with telecommunications and computers.

Even at a young age, Abigail had a noticeable gift for acting. Costars say she is very serious when playing a role.

August 2

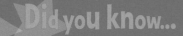
Starting Out

Abigail started acting when she was very young. She was just three when she appeared in a **commercial** for Toys "R" Us. She became a better actress by doing several more commercials.

Abigail's brother Spencer was also discovered at age three! His work as an actor helped Abigail get acting jobs.

The Early Years

In 2002, Abigail appeared in her first movie. It was a science fiction thriller called *Signs*.

Around this time, Abigail had a few small television **roles**, too. She appeared on *Law & Order: Special Victims Unit* and *What I Like About You*.

In *Signs*, Abigail worked with well-known actors Joaquin Phoenix (*left*) and Mel Gibson (*right*). She played the daughter of Mel's character.

Abigail and her brother Spencer acted in *Raising Helen* in 2004. They played **siblings** in the movie.

Raising Helen tells the story of three children who lose their parents. Then, they must live with their aunt Helen. Together, they learn to depend on each other and become a strong family.

Abigail, Spencer, and actress Hayden Panettiere played three siblings in *Raising Helen*.

In *Little Miss Sunshine*, Abigail
worked with actors Toni Collette,
Steve Carell, and Greg Kinnear.

Big Break

In 2006, Abigail starred in *Little Miss Sunshine*. She played Olive Hoover.
In the movie, Olive wants to be in a beauty pageant. The story follows the Hoover family's adventures while driving to the pageant.

Did you know...

Abigail has won more than seven awards for her work in *Little Miss Sunshine*.

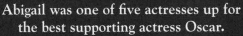
Abigail was one of five actresses up for the best supporting actress Oscar.

In 2007, Abigail was **nominated** for several acting awards for her work in *Little Miss Sunshine*. One was an Academy Award, or Oscar, for best supporting actress. Abigail was the fourth-youngest actress ever nominated for this award.

Abigail didn't win the Oscar. But, it was an honor to be nominated. This honor helped people notice her.

Abigail attended the Oscars in 2007. She said it was fun to meet famous actors and actresses.

After *Little Miss Sunshine*, Abigail was offered **roles** in other movies. In 2007, she appeared in *No Reservations*. In 2008, she acted in *Definitely, Maybe*.

Later that year, Abigail had a starring role as Nim in *Nim's Island*. In the movie, Nim lives on an island with her dad. When her dad gets stuck in a storm, Nim has to survive on her own.

Abigail acted with Jodie Foster and Gerard Butler in *Nim's Island*. Like Abigail, Jodie worked as a child actress.

Making It Big

In 2008, Abigail had the lead **role** in *Kit Kittredge: An American Girl*. The movie is based on a character from the American Girl doll collection.

The story takes place in the 1930s. Abigail's character, Kit, wants to be a newspaper reporter. Kit's family struggles because of the **Great Depression**. Her dad must leave to find work. And, her mom takes in **boarders** and sells eggs for extra money.

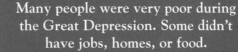

Many people were very poor during the Great Depression. Some didn't have jobs, homes, or food.

Abigail traveled throughout the United States to tell people about her movie.

Many people snapped Abigail's picture at the movie's premiere.

Kit Kittredge: An American Girl was a success! Many girls saw the movie when it opened in July 2008. Some even brought their dolls along!

Did you know...

Actors dress up to attend movie premieres. They invite friends and family to see their movie for the first time. Before the movie, the actors walk down a red carpet. Fans and journalists take pictures of them.

KIT KITTREDGE
An American Girl

ACADEMY AWARD® NOMINEE ABIGAIL BRESLIN IS

O'DONNELL   CUSACK   TUCCI

American Girl

American Girl is a popular brand. It is best known for its dolls. Each of its 14 historical dolls teaches girls about a different American time period. Some of the characters include Molly McIntire, Addy Walker, and Felicity Merriman.

Many children collect American Girl dolls. They can also collect American Girl books, clothing, and magazines.

American Girl Place is the American Girl store. These stores have cafés, live theaters, and even doll hair salons.

Abigail collects American Girl dolls. She owns 13, including Kit Kittredge!

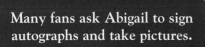

Many fans ask Abigail to sign autographs and take pictures.

Buzz

Abigail wants to continue acting. In 2008, she started working on *My Sister's Keeper*. This movie, based on a book by Jodi Picoult, was expected out in 2009. Fans are excited to see what's next for rising star Abigail Breslin!

Snapshot

★**Name**: Abigail Breslin

★**Birthday**: April 14, 1996

★**Birthplace**: New York City, New York

★**Appearances**: *Signs, Raising Helen, The Princess Diaries 2: Royal Engagement, Little Miss Sunshine, The Santa Clause 3: The Escape Clause, No Reservations, Definitely, Maybe, Nim's Island, Kit Kittredge: An American Girl*

Important Words

beauty pageant (PA-juhnt) a contest between a group of girls or women that often includes a showing of beauty, talent, and character.

boarder a person who pays a fee in exchange for a room, meals, or both.

commercial (kuh-MUHR-shuhl) a short message on television or radio that helps sell a product.

Great Depression the period from 1929 to 1942 of worldwide economic trouble when there was little buying and selling, and many people could not find work.

manager someone who directs the work of a person or a group.

nominate to name as a possible winner.

role a part an actor plays in a show.

sibling a brother or a sister.

telecommunications the science of sending messages over long distances by electronic means, as by telegraph, telephone, television, or computer.

Web Sites

To learn more about Abigail Breslin, visit ABDO Publishing Company online. Web sites about Abigail Breslin are featured on our Book Links page. These links are routinely monitored and updated to provide the most current information available.

www.abdopublishing.com

Index